DAVI
THE FUG
TRUE FRIEN~~~

GW00359985

BOOK 2 (TOLD FROM 1 SAMUEL, 18-20, 22-25, PSALM 27)

TOLD BY CARINE MACKENZIE
~ ILLUSTRATED BY GRAHAM KENNEDY ~

COPYRIGHT © 2009 CARINE MACKENZIE
ISBN 978-1-84550-487-8
PUBLISHED BY CHRISTIAN FOCUS PUBLICATIONS, GEANIES HOUSE,
FEARN, TAIN, ROSS-SHIRE, IV20 1TW, SCOTLAND, U.K.
PRINTED IN CHINA

David was a great hero in Israel but Saul was very jealous of him.

David came to play music to Saul when he was depressed.

Saul was so jealous of David, he flung a spear at him, trying to harm him, but David escaped.

The Lord was with David. This made Saul even more afraid. He wanted to kill David and hoped he would be killed in battle, but God kept him safe.

David had to run away to escape Saul. Michal, his wife, let him down through a window. Michal put a statue in David's bed with goat's hair on the head. Anyone looking in would think David was asleep in bed.

When at last Saul found out that David was far away, he was angry with Michal. Jonathan, Saul's son was a faithful friend to David. They made a covenant, a special promise, to be friends always, no matter what happened.

Saul was very angry that his son Jonathan was a friend of David.

"Don't you realise that you will not be king because of him?"

"But David has done nothing wrong," replied Jonathan. "Why should he be killed?"

Saul flung a spear at Jonathan in anger, trying to kill him.

Jonathan knew that his father was determined to kill David too.

Jonathan warned David of his father's wicked plan. "Take care," he said. "Hide until the morning."

David was able to come back to the king's house to play music to help Saul. Then again Saul grabbed his spear and tried to pin David to the wall. Jonathan and David were still firm friends. "I will help you," he said.

David knew it was not safe to go to King Saul's house. He hid out in the fields.

Jonathan had made an agreement with David. He would warn David of any danger from King Saul.

Jonathan went out to the field with a little servant boy.

"Run and find the arrow I shoot," he told the boy.

Jonathan shot an arrow. As the boy ran to fetch it, Jonathan shouted, "Is the arrow not beyond you?" That was the signal to David that he had to run away.

"Hurry. Do not delay!" shouted Jonathan. The boy was sent back to the city. David appeared from his hiding place.

David and Jonathan renewed their vows of friendship.

David escaped to the cave of Adullam. Some of his family came to join him. People who were in distress and trouble followed David there. Eventually about 400 men were with David.

Saul was still chasing David. David roamed the mountains and wilderness. God kept David safe. Saul was not able to harm him.

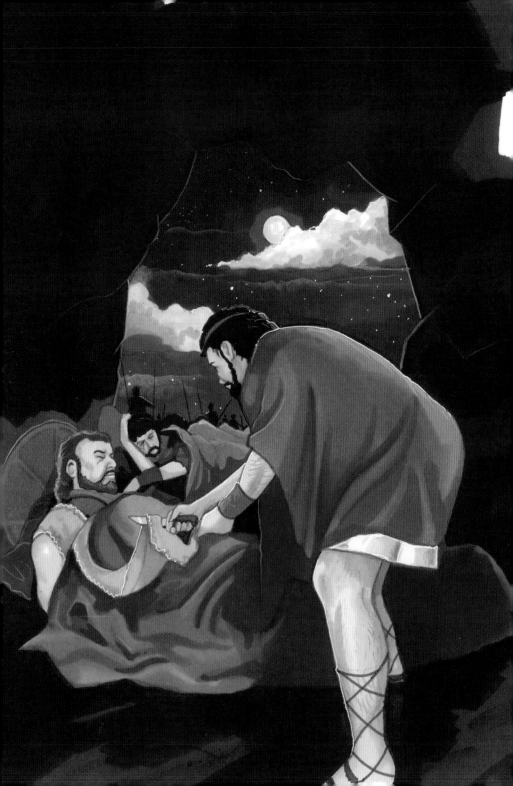

Saul came to the entrance of a cave where David and his men were hiding. David could have easily killed Saul, but he refused to do so. He secretly cut off a corner of Saul's robe.

After Saul left the cave, David shouted after him. "My Lord the king!" Saul turned back.

"I could have killed you today. Look, I have the corner of your robe here. Why do you want to do me harm? I do not want to harm you."

Saul was very moved by David's words. "You are more righteous than I am. You are good to me, even when I am bad to you."

David and his men protected the shepherds of a rich farmer called Nabal. David heard that Nabal was making a feast for his shepherds. He sent a message to Nabal asking if there would be any food for himself and his soldiers.

Nabal refused very ungraciously. David was angry. "Gird on your swords," he told his men.

But before he attacked Nabal and his shepherds, Nabal's wife Abigail arrived.

She had heard what happened. In order to persuade David not to attack she brought a gift of lovely food and wine for David and his men. "Nabal is a fool," she said, "Please forgive us."

Soon after this Nabal died. David asked Abigail to marry him.

Still Saul kept on hunting David. One night they camped near Ziph. David's spies warned him. "Will anyone come down with me to the camp?" David asked. "I will," said Abishai.

At dead of night David and Abishai crept past the guards to where Saul was sleeping.

"You can kill him now with one stroke from his spear," Abishai urged.

"I will not harm the man God has anointed as king," David replied. "He shall die in God's time."

David took the spear and jug of water that were at Saul's head and got away undetected to the other side of the valley. He shouted from the top of the hill, waking up the guards.

"You have not guarded your king very well! Look, I have his spear and water jug!"

Saul recognised David's voice. He realised that David had spared his life again.

Saul seemed to be ashamed of his treatment of David. "I have sinned," he said, "I will harm you no more."

But David knew he was not really safe.

God was in charge of David's life. David could say with confidence, "The Lord is my light and salvation. Why should I be afraid of anything?" (Psalm 27)

Jesus Christ is light and salvation for everyone who trusts in him.

David and Jonathan knew what it was like to be true friends but Jesus Christ is the friend who sticks closer than any brother. Trust in him because he is truly faithful.